Know Your Dogs

Jack
Byard

Old Pond Publishing

First published 2012

Copyright © Jack Byard, 2012

The moral rights of the author in this work have been asserted.

ISBN 978-1-908397-16-4

A catalogue record for this book is available from the British Library

Published by

Old Pond Publishing Ltd
Dencora Business Centre
36 White House Road
Ipswich IP1 5LT
United Kingdom

www.oldpond.com

Book design by Liz Whatling
Printed and bound in China

Contents

Acknowledgements

A great thank you to all the breeders and dog lovers whose help and enthusiasm has been unbelievable. Long telephone conversations and many emails have made me realise how much the owners and breeders truly love their animals. Thanks also to my granddaughter Rebecca who at the weekends keeps me supplied with strong coffee, and to my young friend Sophie whose love of anything with four legs is infectious. Thank you.

To Roger, Heather, George (Georgina), Ellie, Bob and Liz who ensure I do not lead a quiet life.

I suppose I had better say that all mistakes are mine and mine alone; given a chance I would blame Rebecca and Sophie.

Picture Credits

(1) Clydebrook Airedales, *(2)* Danti Akitas, *(3)* Eileen Speich, *(4)* Photo by Thornapple for Applefire Aussies, *(5)* Lesley White and Lesley Moorby www.merrilyn.co.uk, *(6)* Kenneth and Pat Walters, *(7)* Mainline Border Collie Centre, *(8)* Owned by Jan and Mike Hollingsbee, photo by J. Martin, *(9)* Billymart, *(10)* Newlaithe Boxers, *(11)* Golbourne Bulldogs, *(12)* Dawn Inett and Rosemary Harrison, Carradine Cairn Terriers, *(13)* Owned by Rachel Surman, photo by Photocall, *(14)* Lee Humphreys, Amarantos, (15) www.jinglisharpei.co.uk, *(16)* Ch. Sengepabu Saint Valentine owned by Ms Karen Holden, photo by Will Harris, Snap an Image, *(17)* Photo by Jacqueline Smallwood of Lascelles Dalmatians, *(18)* Martin and Jay Horgan, photo Alan Walker, *(19)* www.shutterstock.co.uk, *(20)* Titirangi English Springer Spaniels, *(21)* Sonia Collins, *(22)* Meadowdale Gundogs www.meadowdale.co.uk, *(23)* Sheenagh Gebhard, Calacarey Retrievers, *(24)* Sharandanes (Sharandanes Snow Leopard), *(25)* Mrs Diane Stewart-Richie and Mr Alec Stewart. Photo by Will Harris, *(26)* Dolwen Labradors. Arwyn Ellis, Llwyn, Llanystumdwy, Criccieth, Gwynedd, LL52 0ST *(27)* Dorothy Quelch Ardquin, *(28)* Dave and Karen Gettings, Surianne, *(29)* Lorna Adamo, *(30)* 'Jenson is Loved', owned and bred by Maria and Stephen Cockerham (Yakuza Miniature Schnauzers) *(31)* Luna aka 'Stelamah Just Love Her', photo by Paul Dodd of Essex, *(32)* Margaret Mallows, *(33)* Elessar Corgis, *(34)* Chris Vandeburgt, *(35)* Jane Rowden, Itzapromise Poodles, *(36)* Denise Maxwell, Caerufapugs, *(37)* Di McCann, *(38)* Champion Shelridge Sunshimmer (Cara) bred by Christine Aaron, *(39)* www.shutterstock.co.uk, *(40)* Azgard Kennel, *(41)* Miss Nickson and Sharoc Espirit Santos, *(42)* Lisa & Alec Coull, Callisae Longhaired Weimaraners, *(43)* www.shutterstock.co.uk, *(44)* Mary Anderson, *(45)* Joe Magri and Kevin Arrowsmith, Rozamie and Arrowbien www.rozamiearrowbien.co.uk.

Foreword

Your pet, companion, working or show dog is only a few steps from a wolf on the evolutionary scale and I am not entirely sure when we decided it would be of mutual benefit to work together. In exchange for shelter and a share of the family food dogs would protect us from predators and thieves and keep our homes free from vermin.

Over the years, dogs have taken on many different roles; they were bred to herd, to hunt and to guard. They then became valued as companions and show dogs. Many breeds now serve as therapy dogs as their calming influence gives comfort to the sick or disabled and helps children to read.

To me it is me inconceivable why anyone would breed and train a dog to be a vicious or unstable animal apart from to give the owner a sense of power – when things go wrong it is always the dog that suffers. I have always believed there is no such thing as a naturally bad dog, just bad or irresponsible owners.

If you are considering buying a dog please do not underestimate the amount of time, commitment and training it will require. Dogs are like children, they need rules and boundaries; given these you will have a happy and contented companion.

Jack Byard 2012

I.

Airedale Terrier

Native to:
Yorkshire in the British Isles

Height:
56-61cm (22-24in)

Weight:
25-30kg (55-66lb)

Description

The double-coat is waterproof. The outer-coat is dense and wiry and the under-coat is soft. The back, top of the neck and tail are black or grizzle and the rest is tan. The eyes are dark.

The Airedale, named after the river Aire in West Yorkshire, is the largest of the British terriers. In the 18th century vermin and predators such as rats and otters kept food from the table; the dog developed to solve this problem needed to be smarter, able to hunt on land and water and to scent its prey as well as being the family guard dog.

Before becoming the Airedale Terrier in 1886 the breed was called the Bingley Terrier after a village in the area. The Airedale proved to be a success; it became popular as a hunting dog, a show dog and a pet and has been used by both the police and the military. The energetic Airedale needs lots of exercise. It makes a wonderful family dog but must be trained and socialised from an early age.

2.

Akita

Native to:
Japan

Height:
61-77cm (24-28in)

Weight:
34-54kg (75-110lb)

Description

Akitas can be any colour. Their outer-coat is coarse and straight, standing out from the body and the under-coat is soft and dense. The tail is large and curls over the body. The eyes are dark brown and almond-shaped.

These loyal, intelligent dogs were bred in the Far East from the 17th century until the early 20th century, primarily as fighting dogs and also for hunting in pairs. There are writings in Japan dating back to the 8th century which describe a dog very similar in appearance to the Akita.

In 1934 the Akita was declared a National Monument in Japan in response to declining numbers and in order to preserve the bloodlines which were seen to be threatened by interbreeding with European breeds.

Although the Akita is not for newbies as it has a dominant nature and can be obstinate, with firm handling it will become loyal and cooperative. Their hunting instinct remains and care must be taken around smaller animals.

American Cocker Spaniel

Native to:
America

Height:
37-39cm (14.5-15.5in)

Weight:
7-14kg (15-30lb)

Description

Their medium-length silky coat and feathering are straight or slightly wavy. The head hair is short and fine. The Cocker Spaniel can be parti-coloured (white with patches of black or brown), black, buff or brown, sometimes with tan points.

The Cocker Spaniel arrived in America care of the Pilgrim Fathers on board the *Mayflower* in 1620. Vital for the settlers survival, these dogs retrieved hunted game.

The American Cocker was developed from the English breed and both are used to retrieve game, mainly woodcock and quail. Until the early years of the 20th century the two breed were almost identical in appearance but by the 1940s the differences were becoming more obvious. The American Cocker is slightly smaller than its English cousin with a different shaped head and a longer, thicker coat which make it more often a show-dog or pet than a working animal.

These dogs do not require acres of space but long walks and daily grooming are essential.

Australian Shepherd

Native to:
America

Height:
46-58cm (18-23in)

Weight:
18-29kg (40-65lb)

Description

The Australian Shepherd is black, liver, blue merle or red merle and may have tan points and white markings on the chest, face and legs. The eyes are almond-shaped.

The Aussie was developed in America with origins before that in the Basque region of Spain and France. At some point they were also crossed with collies. It is believed that many flocks of sheep from the Basque region were exported to Australia accompanied by the shepherds and their dogs. During the gold rush of 1849 these shepherds and dogs then travelled to California and it is these Basque dogs from Australia which became Australian Shepherds.

The Aussie is very intelligent and good natured so makes an ideal family dog. This is not a pet for a small apartment or house; it has boundless energy and requires a large amount of physical and mental exercise, without which it will become unhappy and destructive. They are used for detecting narcotics and in search and rescue.

5.

Beagle

Native to:
The British Isles

Height:
33-44cm (13-16in)

Weight:
8-14kg (18-31lb)

Description

The Beagle's coat is short, dense and weatherproof. They are usually black or white with patches of tan, lemon, red, white or black. The eyes are dark brown or hazel.

A Beagle look-a-like was hunting alongside the Greeks in 4,000 BC and was certainly in this country when the Romans invaded. The first written reference to the Beagle was in the 15th century and the dog that we know and love today was developed in the mid 1800s from a mixture of several hounds including the foxhound. It was then refined to create a good-looking dog and a superb hunter. It is recorded that Prince Albert owned a pack of beagles.

The Beagle's sensitive nose keeps it gainfully employed as a sniffer dog at airports for locating certain illegal items. You will also see them at disaster areas sniffing out chemicals used to start and accelerate fires.

Good family dogs, Beagles are easy-going and love being with children.

Bichon Frise

Native to:
Belgium/France

Height:
23-30cm (9-12in)

Weight:
3-5kg (7-12lb)

Description

The hypoallergenic Bichon Frise is snow-white, cream, grey or apricot. Their outer-coat is coarse, curly and 7-10cm (3-4in) long. The under-coat is soft and dense. The tail is well-covered and curls over the back. The nose is black and the eyes are round, black or dark brown.

The origins of the Bichon Frise are obscure but there is documentation of traders in the years BC having small white dogs which may be ancestors of the Bichon Frise. In the 15th century the Bichon Frise became popular with European nobility, Henry III kept his in a basket around his neck. Within 200 years, life for the Bichon was turned upside down and from being a pampered companion of the rich and famous they had become a 'common' street dog, popular with organ grinders and circuses.

This is a small but energetic dog that requires a daily walk and a good safe place where they can play to burn off their surplus energy.

Border Collie

Native to:
The British Isles

Height:
53cm (22in) on average

Weight:
12-20kg (27-45lb)

Description

Border Collies can be one of many colours or combinations of colours. Their eyes are deep brown, amber or blue.

The Border Collie is a descendant of the droving dogs bred along the English/Scottish border. The Border Collie as we know it today appeared at the end of the 1800s. A great number of the best of the breed can be traced to a dog called Old Hemp born in 1893. Old Hemp had all the qualities of a good Border Collie and many local shepherds used him to breed their own dogs.

The Border Collie is highly intelligent and enjoys working with people. Their intelligence makes them ideal for work other than herding such as searching for drugs and explosives or search and rescue.

They need ample time to exercise their bodies and minds. They will chew their way through your home, leave your garden looking like a lunar landscape and attempt to herd children and other pets.

8.

Border Terrier

Native to:
The Scottish and Northumbrian borders in the British Isles

Height:
28-31cm (11-12in)

Weight:
5-7kg (11-15lb)

Description

Border Terriers can be red, wheaten and grizzle or blue and tan. Grey mixed with the coat colour gives a tweed effect. The harsh, wiry outer-coat is weather- and dirt-resistant. The under-coat is much softer. They have an otter-shaped head and their eyes are dark.

These sturdy little terriers are no-frills working dogs.

The Border Terrier can trace its beginnings to the 1700s and in the intervening years it has changed very little. The border farmers kept these terriers to dispatch foxes and vermin which were stealing game fowl and sheep. They will also clear an area of rats, mice, rabbits and squirrels.

They are ideal family pets suitable for any size of home. However, this is an active, intelligent dog that needs both mental and physical stimulation with two hours exercise a day. Good training is a must as they will chase any small animal, risking life and limb.

Boston Terrier

Native to:
America

Height:
38-43cm (15-17in)

Weight:
4.5-11.5kg (12-23.3lb)

Description

Boston Terriers are brindle, black with white markings or seal. The eyes are round and dark.

The Boston Terrier, nicknamed 'the American Gentleman', was the first purebred dog to be developed in America. It is believed it was bred from a fighting dog, said to be an imported English bulldog called Hooper's Judge, which was crossed with an English White Terrier. The resulting pups were the ancestors of the modern Boston Terrier. All Boston Terriers have evolved from these two dogs. Bred originally for ratting and possibly fighting, they once weighed in at a massive 20kg (44lb) though the modern version has been slimmed down.

By 1889 the popularity of the breed had grown and enthusiasts formed the American Bull Terrier Club but this did not go down well with Bull Terrier breeders and in 1891 it was renamed the Boston Terrier Club. This cheerful character is an ideal family companion.

Boxer

Native to:
Germany

Height:
53-63cm (21-25in)

Weight:
27-29kg (53-70lb)

Description

The coat is short, smooth and shiny; the colours are fawn and brindle and both vary in shade. All can have white markings. The eyes are dark brown.

The Boxer is a cross of the German Bullenbeisser (now extinct), the Mastiff and the Bulldog and was custom-bred for hunting. The shape of the face and jaws, the position and shape of the nose and even the creases in their cheeks are all part of the design. These powerful dogs would hold the prey until the hunter arrived. They were used in dog fighting, bull-baiting and as cattle dogs as well as in circuses and theatres since they are quick to learn.

The modern Boxer is highly intelligent, playful and curious. If your Boxer is trained and socialised from an early age it will be happy in human and other animal company, although chickens may be a step too far. Plenty of daily physical and mental exercise are needed. They love attention and can become destructive if left alone for too long.

Bulldog

Native to:
The British Isles

Height:
31-40cm (12-16in)

Weight:
22-25kg (49-55lb)

Description

The coat is short, fine and sleek. Bulldog colours include brindle, red, fawn or white, either as single colour or a combination. Their eyes are round and dark, almost black.

The Bulldog is believed to date back to before the 16th century and the name Bulldog was first recorded in the 1630s. The 'Bull' was adopted because they were used in the sport of bull-baiting which made illegal in 1835. The dogs were bred for appearance when their fighting qualities were no longer required and breeders have worked hard to remove the aggression. Modern Bulldogs bear little resemblance to the original.

To all appearances this dog is one tough cookie, a solid, well-muscled animal with a world-weary face. They are, in fact, the most friendly and gentle of breeds, good with children and an ideal companion who will guard its human family. The American breed is taller and has a longer muzzle; the French version is shorter and not as stocky.

Cairn Terrier

Native to:
Scotland

Height:
28-31cm (11-12in)

Weight:
6-8kg (13-17lb)

Description

The Cairn Terrier can be cream, wheaten, red, grey or brindle. They have a harsh weather-resistant outer-coat with a short soft under-coat. The eyes are dark hazel with shaggy eyebrows.

The Cairn Terrier was originally developed on the Isle of Skye and is a mix of the original working terriers of the highlands and islands of Scotland. The Scottish King James VI made a gift of a number of terriers, believed to be the forbears of the Cairn, to King Charles IX of France. They were so highly prized that groups were sent on separate ships to avoid possible English Channel disasters.

This is one of the oldest terrier breeds and gained its name for hunting its prey amongst the cairns in the Scottish Highlands. The terriers were used by crofters and shepherds to control vermin such as mice, rats, rabbits and even foxes.

They are intelligent, feisty and make an ideal family dog and mouser.

Cavalier King Charles Spaniel

Native to:
The British Isles

Height:
30-33cm (12-13in)

Weight:
5.9-8.2kg (13-18lb)

Description

They have a medium-length silky coat which is black-and-tan, ruby, Blenheim or tricolour. The eyes are large and dark.

Named after King Charles II, the Cavalier King Charles Spaniel (Cavie) is descended from the King Charles Spaniel. In the late 1600s the King Charles was interbred with Pugs to create the breed we know today. In 1926 Roswell Eldridge offered £25, almost £1,200 today, to anyone who could reproduce the long-nosed breed which was popular in the reign of Charles II. The prize was won by Miss Mostyn Walker, but unfortunately Roswell had died a few months before and never saw his dream come true.

In 1940 the new variety was recognised as a separate breed and 'Cavalier' was added to the name to distinguish the new breed from its ancestors: the Cavalier King Charles Spaniel had arrived. The Cavie is intelligent and enjoys a good cuddle; a guard dog it will never be. They have been known to chase everything from a mouse to a Rolls Royce.

Chihuahua

Native to:
America

Height:
15-23cm (6-10in)

Weight:
Up to 3kg (up to 6lb)

Description

The Chihuahua's coat can be long, short, wavy or smooth and is black, white, chestnut, fawn, sand, sable, steel blue, black or tan. The ears are large and erect and the eyes are dark, large and round.

The Chihuahua is named after a state in Mexico but its history is almost impossible to confirm. It has appeared in America, Mexico, Spain, China, Malta and a fresco painted by Botticelli in the Sistine Chapel in Rome, all before the discovery of the New World. It is certainly one of the oldest breeds in the world. The ancestors of the Chihuahua (often know as 'Chis') are almost as difficult to pin down as its country of origin. Some evidence suggests they existed in South America long before the Mayans where they were kept as companion dogs and for religious ceremonies.

The Chi is a naturally small, one-man dog which tends to be distrustful so not an ideal family companion. It may be small but regular exercise is a necessity.

Chinese Shar Pei

Native to:
China

Height:
48-51cm (18-21in)

Weight:
18-25kg (40-55lb)

Description

The Shar Pei's harsh, bristly coat can be any colour except white. The tail is tightly curled and the eyes are dark.

Several areas of China and Thailand are given as the Shar Pei's birth place. When the communists came to power in China many documents about the Shar Pei's history were destroyed, making it difficult to trace. They are possibly related to the Chow Chow since both have blue mouths.

Images of a dog with superb wrinkles can be seen on pottery of the Han Dynasty from 206 BC and a 2nd century AD statue of a Shar Pei can be seen in the Boston Fine Art Museum. The Shar Pei was bred for hunting, herding and guarding. They were also used in dog fighting and it is believed that their wrinkled skin and harsh hair protected them from serious injury.

This is a dog for the experienced owner; they need a firm but fair hand. If the dog does not see you as the pack leader they can become stubborn and refuse to do as required.

Dachshund (Longhaired)

Native to:
Germany

Height:
20-27cm (8-11in)

Weight:
4.5-5kg (10-11lb)

Description

The Dachsund has a dense, smooth coat and the skin should be loose and supple. They are any colour except white. The eyes are dark and almond-shaped.

A mummified Dachshund-type dog was found in a burial urn in the 5,000-year-old tomb of a Pharoah. It is difficult to trace a family tree for the breed but it may include: German Shorthaired Pointer; Pinscher; St Hubert and Bassett Hound.

The modern Dachshund was developed in Germany in the 17th century where it was used for hunting rabbits, stoats, foxes and badgers ('dachs' being the German word for badger). The long floppy ears were developed to stop dirt and seeds getting in and the strong curly tail, I am told, was used to pull them out of a burrow if they got stuck.

Though some Dachshunds are still used for hunting, the majority are companions. They are affectionate and intelligent but strong-willed. Forty minutes exercise a day will keep you and the dog happy and healthy.

Dalmatian

Native to:
Croatia

Height:
56-61cm (22-24in)

Weight:
16-32kg (35-70lb)

Description

Their coat is short, hard, dense and glossy. The preferred colour is white with well-defined black or brown spots. The eyes are oval.

This is an ancient breed by anybody's standards; spotted dogs are depicted on ancient Egyptian decorations dating back 2,500 years and a similar breed known as the Bengal pointer was known to exist in the British Isles in the 18th century. The Dalmatian is an excellent guard dog and was once used as a war dog for guarding the national borders. In the 19th century they were used as carriage dogs, clearing vermin and other dogs out of the way to give the carriage a clear run. They would then guard the carriage and horse while the master was away.

The Dalmatians come into this world as balls of white fluff; the spots develop as they grow. They have boundless energy, love companionship and playing, and make a happy companion if given plenty of exercise.

Dobermann

Native to:
Germany

Height:
63-72cm (25-28in)

Weight:
32-45kg (71-99lb)

Description

The coat is short and smooth and most commonly black or brown with tan or rust-red markings. In black dogs the eyes are dark brown; in the other colours the eye must be no lighter than the markings.

The Dobermann is a relatively young breed bred by tax collector Herr Dobermann specifically to protect himself and the collected taxes. Apart from being excellent guard dogs they were also used in hunting and killing vermin.

The Dobermann is not a dangerous dog; problems occur due to irresponsible or inexperienced owners. Training your Dobermann will take a great deal of time and patience. They must be trained and socialised from an early age; from the outset you are the pack leader, and this must never change. They make loyal and affectionate companions but are possibly better in a home with older children. A mature dog requires two hours exercise a day; otherwise they will get into mischief, leading to bad behaviour.

English Mastiff

Native to:
The British Isles

Height:
76cm (30in) average

Weight:
68-72kg (150-160lb)

Description

The English Mastiff is a shade of fawn with black on the muzzle and around the eyes.

This is the oldest British breed with ancestors dating back over 2,500 years. It is believed they arrived in the British Isles care of Phoenician traders and were traded for metal ore.

In Feudal Britain some serfs in each village were required by the landowner to keep a Mastiff to reduce the number of wolves, wild hogs and other unwelcome wild beasts. They were also used for bull- and bear-baiting. There is a story that an English Mastiff was taken to America on the *Mayflower* but evidence suggests the breed reached America more towards the end of the 19th century.

Despite its size and strength the English Mastiff is gentle and easy-going. However, it is a born guard dog so it is very important that it is properly trained and socialised from an early age. It is too large to be allowed to become dominant.

English Springer Spaniel

Native to:
The British Isles

Height:
48-51cm (19-20in)

Weight:
23-25kg (51-55lb)

Description

The Springer Spaniel has a short, weather-resistant coat which is a combination of black, dark brown, white or tan. The eyes are hazel and almond-shaped.

The ancestors of all spaniels come from Spain, probably arriving in the British Isles with the Roman invaders in 54-55 BC. From the 17th century spaniels started to be selected by size. The largest animals became the ancestors of the Springer Spaniel and the smaller ones the ancestors of Cocker Spaniels. Thomas Bewick was the first to name the different types and in 1892 the Kennel Club recognised them as separate breeds. The first modern English Springer was bred by the Boughey family of Shropshire.

Apart from their prowess at springing birds into the air for hunters, they are used as sniffer dogs. Merlin (pictured) is an expert in finding firearms and explosives. Springer Spaniels love the outdoors and make wonderful pets. They bubble over with energy, so need plenty of exercise to channel it.

21

German Shepherd

Native to:
Germany

Height:
60-65cm (21-26in)

Weight:
32-40kg (71-88lb)

Description

Most commonly German Shepherds are black or black with tan, red, cream, silver, white or blue. The eyes are brown.

In 1899 a German gentleman by the name of Max von Stephanitz visited a dog show and was shown a dog with the grand name of Hektor Linksrhein. He saw that Hektor was everything a working dog should be and was so impressed that he bought Hektor and founded the Society for the German Shepherd dog. Hektor was to become the basis of the modern German Shepherd which, and as its name suggests, was used for guarding and herding sheep. After World War I the breed was renamed the Alsatian but in 1977 it reverted to its original name.

Highly loyal with an intelligence surpassed only by the Border Collie and the Poodle. These traits make it ideal for use with the military, the police, search and rescue and as a guard dog. Possibly the most versatile dog ever, there are few tasks that a German Shepherd cannot perform.

22

German Shorthaired Pointer

Native to:
Germany

Height:
53-64cm (21-25in)

Weight:
20-32kg (44-70lb)

Description

The coat is short and flat with a dense under-coat and a covering of stiff hair making it water resistant. They can be liver, liver-and-white, black or black-and-white, sometimes with speckles. The feet are webbed.

The German Shorthaired Pointer is a mixture of many hounds and tracker dogs including the English and Spanish Pointers. Prince Albrecht zu Solms-Braunfels of the Royal House of Hanover recommended the breeds that created it. The breed was officially recognised in 1870.

This intelligent breed is calm, loyal and ideal as a family dog. These are working dogs and need to be active with at least one hour's exercise a day plus plenty of mental stimulation. They have been known, when bored, to clear a 2-metre fence to exercise on their own.

The German Shorthaired Pointer is bred to be independent. When out of sight or hearing of its handler instinct takes over and it will think for itself.

23

Golden Retriever

Native to:

The Scottish Highlands

Height:

51-56cm (20-24in)

Weight:

25-36kg (66-70lb)

Description

The coat is dense, firm and water resistant and can be straight or wavy. The underneath is feathered. The colours are from light cream to dark gold. The eyes are dark brown.

This beautiful, intelligent breed was developed in the Scottish Highlands near Glen Affric by Sir Dudley Marjoribanks. All the dogs used to create the breed were sporting dogs. The now extinct Tweed Water Spaniel was crossed with a yellow retriever; the four pups produced were in turn crossed with an Irish Setter, a sandy bloodhound and a St Johns Water Dog. In 1903 the Golden Retriever was registered with the Kennel Club.

These friendly, gentle dogs are far too trusting to be good guard dogs. They are patient, even with children, full of fun and love water and exercise. This hardworking breed is used in many roles as well as retrieving; their calm behaviour makes them ideal for search and rescue and in drug detection.

24

Great Dane

Native to:

Asia

Height:

76cm (30in) minimum

Weight:

45-90kg (100-200lb)

Description

Great Danes are fawn, brindle, blue, black, harlequin or mantle. The colour of the eyes and nose depend on the coat colour.

This gentle giant is said to have started life in Asia. Images of dogs similar to the Great Dane can be found on Greek coinage dating back over 2,000 years and in drawings on Egyptian monuments over 5,000 years old. The breed arrived in Europe in 407 AD when Asian armies invaded Germany, Spain and Italy. Their great size and strength were put to use for hunting wild boar. It has nothing to do with Denmark.

The Great Dane as we know it today is a cross between the original Asian Mastiff, the Wolfhound, the old English Mastiff and the Irish Greyhound and was officially recognised in 1837. Though they are great hunters, trackers and watchdogs they are now mainly kept as companions. The largest one is in America and measures 1.09m (43in) from ground to shoulder and weighs in at 111kg (245lb).

25

Irish Setter

Native to:
Ireland

Height:
64-69cm (25-27in)

Weight:
27-33kg (60-71lb)

Description

Their flat, silky coat is rich chestnut to mahogany, their nose is black or brown and the eyes are almond-shaped.

The Irish Setter was developed in Ireland in the 18th century. A mixture of the Irish Water Spaniel, the English Setter, the Irish Terrier and the Gordon Setter, they were initially bred for hunting, setting and locating upland game birds. Moving with great stealth they locate the game and then wait until the hunter arrives.

Irish Setters are frequently used as therapy dogs in reading programmes; the dogs sit with the children who read to them without being corrected or judged. It is a calm, relaxed atmosphere that benefits the child's progress.

These gentle creatures have been described as rambunctious and eternal puppies. Early obedience training is a must. They are slow to mature but they are also independent and stubborn. Great patience is needed, plus two hours exercise a day.

26

Labrador

Native to:
The British Isles

Height:
55-62cm (21.5-23.5in)

Weight:
25-34kg (55-75lb)

Description

The short, dense and water-resistant coat is black, yellow (from cream to foxy red) or chocolate.

The Labrador's ancestor was the St John's Water Dog of Newfoundland, which, in turn, is a mixture of Portuguese, Irish and English working dogs brought to Newfoundland by the fishermen of these nations.

The St John's Water Dog (now extinct) was well known in this country long before the Earl of Malmesbury obtained some from Newfoundland. The Earl had seen them working on fishing boats and was impressed with their ability to retrieve on land and in water. He used these dogs to create the Labrador and a breed standard.

This is an intelligent, active and gentle animal. As always, training must begin when the dog is young and they must be exercised both mentally and physically. The Labrador makes an ideal pet and is good with children. They can eat for an army so over-feeding can be a problem.

27

Lhasa Apso

Native to:
Tibet

Height:
23-28cm (9-11in)

Weight:
5-8kg (12-18lb)

Description

The Lhasa Apso's dense double-coat is long, straight and heavy. The most popular colours are gold, coral and honey; other colours are slate, smoke, grizzle or multi-coloured. The oval eyes are dark brown.

Originating in Tibet over 4,000 years ago, the Lhasa Apso is one of the oldest dog breeds. The name is taken from 'Lhasa' after the city and 'Apso' meaning long-haired or bearded. Domestication was begun by the Tibetan monks who used them as indoor guard dogs which would bark and alert the outdoor guard dogs, usually Tibetan Mastiffs. It was believed that when a lama died his soul would enter the body of the dog while it waited for reincarnation; so the dogs were never sold and the only way to own one was to receive it as a gift. In the early 20th century they arrived in the British Isles with soldiers returning from India.

Small they may be, but a good walk and a dash around in a secure place will help to keep them healthy.

28

Maltese

Native to:
Malta

Height:
21-23cm (8-10in)

Weight:
3-4kg (6.5-9lb)

Description

Their coat is long, straight, silky and parted down the centre of the spine. Pure white, occasionally with lemon-coloured markings on the ears. The eyes are dark brown and oval with dark rims.

This ancient breed has been well documented down the years from Aristotle in 370 BC to Queen Elizabeth I. Charles Darwin puts the origin of the breed at 6,000 BC. Many believe it originated in Melita, a Sicilian town no longer in existence, while others think it was developed from the Spitz breed in the Swiss mountain villages. Attempts in the 18th century to breed a smaller dog almost destroyed the breed. It is believed the first Maltese dogs to arrive in this country were brought by the crusaders.

This small dog with a built-in cuddle must be trained and socialised from an early age to avoid a snappish bad-tempered pet. Malteses require a good walk, every day. The skin by the parting is prone to sunburn, so take care.

29

Miniature Pinscher

Native to:
Germany

Height:
25-30cm (10-12in)

Weight:
4-5kg (8-10lb)

Description

Their coat is lustrous, smooth, short and hard. The colours are red, black, brown or blue with well-defined tan points. Occasionally they have a white chest patch. The eyes are slightly oval and very dark.

The Miniature Pinscher (the Min Pin), is not a miniature Dobermann; it was around in the 17th century while the Dobermann did not wag a tail until the 19th. It is an ancient breed, although documentation did not start until about 200 years ago, and is generally accepted to be a cross between the Italian Greyhound and the Dachshund. It is a dog bred to work; they would have lived in barns and stables to keep the vermin populations under control.

The Min Pin does not demand acres of space but a daily walk is a must. They have to be taught who is boss and if they have an outdoor area make certain it is secure: they make Houdini look like an amateur. Possibly not an ideal companion in a house with young children.

30

Miniature Schnauzer

Native to:
Germany

Height:
33-35cm (13-14in)

Weight:
7-8kg (15-18lb)

Description

They are double-coated, the outer-coat short harsh and wiry, the under-coat soft and dense. The colours are black, white, salt-and-pepper and black-and-silver. The oval eyes are dark.

The Miniature Schnauzer appeared officially in 1888 but it is believed that the breed has been around for about 600 years. It is a cross between the Standard Schnauzer, the Poodle and the Affenpinscher.

The hair on the body is trimmed but that on the legs, ears and under-body is allowed to grow long; they have bushy beards, moustaches and large eyebrows.

Miniature Schnauzers were bred to be ratters. If they are not properly trained small pets, cats, mice and birds will be seen as fair game to this intelligent hunter. They make excellent companions which will sleep on your bed and make excellent guard dogs. They have high energy and love going for walks and playing which will make them happy, well-behaved companions.

31

Newfoundland

Native to:
Newfoundland

Height:
59- 74cm (27-29in)

Weight:
45-68kg (100-150lb)

Description

They are black, brown, grey or black and white. The outer-coat is oily, flat and water-resistant; the under-coat is oily and dense. They have dark brown eyes and webbed feet.

It is one belief, amongst others, that Newfoundlands are descendants of a breed brought to the colony of Newfoundland by the Vikings. Many crosses later we have the modern Newfoundland.

The Newfie is the gentlest of giants and was used for hauling in fishing nets and rescuing anybody or anything that fell into the water; they also pulled mail carts, milk floats and, in WWII, sledges of ammunition and other supplies in Alaskan blizzards.

In 1919 a Newfie pulled a lifeboat carrying 20 shipwrecked survivors to safety and was awarded a gold medal.

They are intelligent, calm and love children. Early training is a must as is good daily exercise and an occasional swim.

Pekingese

Native to:
China

Height:
15-23cm (6-9in)

Weight:
3.2-6.4kg (7-14lb)

Description

The Pekingese has a double-coat; the outer-coat is thick, coarse and long, the under-coat is thick and soft. They can be any colour. The hair is feathered on the back of the legs, ears, tail and toes. The eyes are dark and round.

The breed is over 4,000 years old and is named after the ancient city of Peking (Beijing) where it was worshipped in the temples. The breed could only be owned by members of the Chinese Imperial Palace and stealing or injuring one was punishable by death. Four Pekingese would walk before the Emperor announcing his arrival by barking.

In 1860, during the Second Opium War, the Forbidden City was under British and French occupation. Sir John Fitzroy obtained two dogs which he gave to the Duke and Duchess of Richmond. They became the basis of the Pekingese in Britain.

The Peke is brave, independent, sensitive and affectionate so they make excellent companions.

33

Pembroke Welsh Corgi

Native to:
Wales

Height:
25-30cm (10-12in)

Weight:
9-12 kg (20-26lb)

Description

Corgis are red-and-white, tri-colour or sable, occasionally with white markings on the legs, chest, face or neck. The eyes are medium brown.

There are two types of Welsh Corgi, the Pembroke and the Cardigan, both named after the Welsh counties. Queen Elizabeth II is the most prominent owner of Pembroke Corgi which have been Royal companions for over 70 years. They have a head which is fox-like in appearance and tend to be more gregarious than their Cardigan cousins.

Developed as herding dogs, the Pembroke is believed to have been introduced into Wales by Flemish weavers some time between 920 and 1100 AD. Corgis herd cattle by nipping their heels to drive them forward. Their size prevent them from being kicked. If a cow turns around to confront it tormentor it will receive a swift nip on the nose.

This hardy and intelligent breed is full of fun, even-tempered and happier with older children.

34

Pomeranian

Native to:
Germany/Poland

Height:
18-30cm (7-12in)

Weight:
1-3kg (3-7lb)

Description

The Pomeranian is double-coated; the outer-coat is long, straight, and harsh; the under-coat is short and dense. They are white, black, light and dark brown or pale blue. The slightly oval eyes are dark brown and the well-covered tail is carried over the back.

The Pom was developed in Pomerania which is now a part of northern Poland and eastern Germany. This diminutive dog is a descendant of the Spitz which originated from arctic regions. The original Pomeranians were much larger than their modern cousins, weighing in at a mighty 14-23kg (30-50lb), and were used for herding sheep. In 1888 Queen Victoria imported a Pomeranian from Florence and spent a great deal of effort developing the breed. During her reign the breed became 50 per cent smaller.

This dog is a cocky extrovert with a built-in cuddle factor. Give plenty of training and regular grooming and you will have an affectionate companion.

Poodle
(Standard)

Native to:
Germany

Height:
38cm (15in)

Weight:
21-35kg (46-77lb)

Description

The Poodle's coat is dense and curly and can be black, white, blue, grey, silver, brown, apricot or cream. The colours will start to fade at 4 or 5 years of age. The eyes are dark and almond-shaped eyes.

The Poodle has been around since the 15th and 16th centuries. Although it is universally thought to be French, its origins are in Germany where they are known as Pudel. It is believed that the Poodle we know today was developed in the 1600s. The miniature and toy breeds followed shortly after and were very popular pets from 1700 to the late 1800s. Poodles are excellent swimmers and their water-resistant coat makes them ideal for retrieving game fowl from the water.

This intelligent, lively dog loves children and being the centre of attention. They need up to one and a half hours exercise a day and an occasional swim. They love to play fetch, followed by a nap on the settee.

36

Pug

Native to:
China

Height:
25-36cm (10-14in)

Weight:
6-9kg (13-20lb)

Description

The Pug's coat is smooth and fawn or black. The head is large and round, the ears are small, thin and velvety. The muzzle is short and blunt and the large face has large wrinkles. The eyes are prominent and dark.

There is evidence that the Pug was around in 400 BC. It is believed that Tibetan monks kept them as pets and the Chinese used them to guard temples. According to research, the Pug arrived in Europe with sailors of the Dutch East India Company who could not resist this wrinkly-faced dog.

One Pug, thought to be called Pompey, saved the life of William I, the founder of the Netherlands. In 1592 the Dutch camp was about to be attacked by Spanish forces, the brave Pug woke William I and saved the day.

Napoleon and Josephine had a pet Pug. In 1714 one joined Hogarth in a self portrait. Queen Victoria bred several and we all know the cigar-smoking Pug in *Men in Black*.

37

Rottweiler

Native to:
Germany

Height:
63-76cm (23.5-30in)

Weight:
36-54kg (80-120lb)

Description

Rottweilers are black with clearly-defined rust, rich tan or mahogany markings on the eyes, cheeks, muzzle, chest, feet and beneath the tail. The outer-coat is coarse, straight and dense. There are black lines on the toes.

Arriving in Germany with the Roman eleventh legion in 74 AD into Rottweil (meaning 'red villa'), these powerful, intelligent dogs were used to herd cattle and guard them against wolves and bears. The Rottie has also been used for herding ducks and geese and pulling dog carts.

German migrants and American travellers brought Rottweiler to America and the breed was listed with the American Kennel Club in 1931. They came to Great Britain after WWII, brought from Germany as guard dogs by servicemen.

Proper training and socialising are essential but despite their size they are a gentle breed and are used frequently as therapy dogs. Lack of training for the dogs and owners has given this breed a reputation it does not deserve.

38

Shetland Sheepdog

Native to:
The Shetland Isles

Height:
33-40.6cm (13-16in)

Weight:
6.4-12.3kg (14-22lb)

Description

Their long outer-coat is straight and harsh; the under-coat is short, soft and dense. The colours are sable, tricolour and blue merle with varying amounts of white and tan or both. The almond-shaped eyes are dark or sometimes blue.

It will come as no surprise that the Shetland Sheepdog is a herding breed. It is descended from the Rough Collie and the Border Collie as well as the Icelandic Yakking (now extinct) which was brought to the islands by fishermen. The breed has changed very little since the 18th century.

It is said they are in tune with their owner's moods and will frequently respond to a command before it has left their lips. The owners I have spoken to cannot give the Sheltie enough praise and describe them as loyal, gentle and loving. The Sheltie is, in fact, an ideal companion and an excellent guard dog. Having said that, the Sheltie still requires training and socialising; they need someone to look up to and that is you. Do not let them down.

39

Shih Tzu

Native to:
China

Height:
28cm (11in)

Weight:
4-7kg (19-16lb)

Description

They have a long, soft, double-coat and a good-sized beard and moustache. They are any colour, usually with a white blaze on the forehead and a white tip to the well-covered tail which is carried over the back.

This small, energetic dog's ancestors go back many thousands of years. Recent research using the very latest technology puts the Shih Tzu in a group of ancient breeds which are close relations to the wolf and includes the Tibetan Lhasa Apso and the Pekingese. These intelligent dogs were once the companions of emperors. I have heard this beautiful breed described as a Chrysanthemum dog because of the shape of its head.

The Shih Tzu is the perfect companion; it will sit with you and allow you to pet and pamper it to your heart's content. Barking, bad or snappish behaviour can, with gentle and constant training, be avoided.

40

Siberian Husky

Native to:
Russia

Height:
51-60cm (20-23.5 in)

Weight:
16-27kg (35-60lb)

Description

Their double-coat usually ranges from black to white. The well-covered tail curves over the back. The almond-shaped eyes are blue, brown or one of each. The large feet act like snow shoes.

The Siberian Husky, Samoyed and Alaskan Malamute are all descended from the dogs that were found in inhospitable places such as Siberia, Alaska, Greenland and Baffin Island.

The Siberian Husky gained worldwide attention in 1925 when the remote village of Nome in Alaska had a diphtheria epidemic and the only way to get vaccines to the stricken village was by dog sled. Teams of Siberian Huskies and mushers carried the medical supplies over 600 miles and saved hundreds of lives.

The Siberian Husky loves human company and physical and mental exercise; lack of either could mean your furniture being chewed by an unhappy dog. They need a strong leader and a weak one will be completely ignored.

41

Staffordshire Bull Terrier

Native to:
The British Isles

Height:
33-41cm (13-16in)

Weight:
10-17kg (23-38lb)

Description

The smooth, short coat is red, fawn, black, white or blue and all can have white markings. The eyes are dark and round.

The Staffy has been around since the 1600s and is a cross between the Bulldog and contemporary terriers. Their main role was in the 'sport' of bull- and bear-baiting and sometimes they were even pitted against each other. After this was outlawed in 1835, the Staffy was used for hunting badgers and clearing areas of vermin.

If you want a quiet, genteel companion then this breed is not for you; everything is done at full speed and with boundless enthusiasm. They need plenty of exercise, a good daily walk and lots of play. This is not a guard dog, they trust everyone and as a result become victims of dog-napping.

Forget all you have heard about the Staffy. This is a highly intelligent and affectionate dog which is good with children. The only problem with a Staffy is an irresponsible owner.

42

Weimaraner (Longhaired)

Native to:
Germany

Height:
56-69cm (22-27in)

Weight:
23-32kg (50-70lb)

Description

The Weimaraner's coat is smooth and silver grey with shades of mouse or rose grey. The long-haired coat is 2.5-5cm (1-2in) long but otherwise identical to the shorthaired. Occasionally they have a black stripe along the back. The eyes are round and are blue-grey or shades of amber.

The breed was developed in the 16th and 17th centuries but records exist of similar dogs at the court of Louis IX of France in the 13th century. It was used in the hunting of bears, wild boar and deer and in later years for smaller game. The long-haired Weimaraner appeared in 1973.

The Weimaraner was bred not only to be a hunting dog but also a family companion. Today the breed craves companionship so to have a happy dog it is essential they are surrounded by the family they want to protect. These are fast, sturdy and intelligent dogs that require plenty of exercise and firm but gentle training from an early age.

43

West Highland White Terrier

Native to:
Scotland

Height:
25-30cm (10-12in)

Weight:
7-10kg (15-22lb)

Description

They are white and double-coated; the outer-coat is straight and hard, the under-coat is soft and dense. The almond-shaped eyes are dark brown.

The West Highland White Terrier (Westie) originated in Poltalloch Argyllshire in Scotland. Scottish white terriers have been around since the 16th and 17th century and it is possible that these are descendants of a cross with Spanish white terriers shipwrecked off the coast of Skye in 1588.

Originally called the Poltalloch Terrier and later the Rosenheath Terrier after the Duke of Argyll's estate on which they were bred. The Duke is said to have decided to have only white terriers after he fatally mistook a reddish-brown one for the fox.

Originally used for ratting, hunting foxes and otters, the hunting and digging instinct is still there. Full of life and affection, this intelligent breed can have a naughty streak so their training must be constantly and gently reinforced.

44

Whippet

Native to:
The British Isles

Height:
55cm (21.5in)

Weight:
11-21kg (25-45lb)

Description

The Whippet's fine, close-textured coat can be any colour or mixture of colours.

Developed in the north of England in the mid to late 1800s, the Whippet was a favourite of colliers and factory workers.

A cross of the Greyhound, the Italian Greyhound and terriers, the first mention of the breed in England was in the early 17th century. Whippet racing was once more popular than football and in the 1800s was a national sport. The breed was recognised by the British Kennel Club in 1890 and the American Kennel Club two years earlier.

This gentle, friendly dog is easy to train. If used as a guard dog they will lick an intruder to death but give them the task they were bred for, coursing or racing, then their courage and stamina are amazing.

They make loving, if highly strung, companions – their primary role today.

45

Yorkshire Terrier

Native to:
The British Isles

Height:
18-20cm (7-8in)

Weight:
2-3kg (4-7lb)

Description

They have beautiful flowing golden-tan hair, similar to human hair. The back is steel blue, the pricked ears are tan and the eyes are round and black.

The industrial revolution brought many changes to the lives of people in Yorkshire and Lancashire. There was plenty of work and many people walked from Scotland to take advantage of it. The Scots brought with them their Scottish terriers which were a mix of Skye, Paisley and Clydesdale terriers and subsequently crossed with the local breeds to create the Yorkie. These feisty working dogs were used in the coal mines, mills and factories to clear them of vermin.

Today's Yorkie bears little resemblance to the Yorkie of the 19th century which weighed almost 14kg (30lb), four times the weight of the modern breed. These dogs are small in stature only and so must to be taught to respect the size and strength of larger animals. They make ideal pets for adults and older children.

Dog Talk

Double-Coat – Having a long outer-coat which is water resistant, and a soft under-coat.
Droving – The practice of moving livestock over large distances on foot with the aid of dogs.
Hypoallergenic – Having a reduced chance of causing an allergic reaction.

Appearance

Blenheim – White background with mahogany markings
Blue Merle – Marbled black, white and grey
Brindle – Black stripes over a fawn background
Feathering – Longer silky hair on the legs and belly
Grizzle – Black mixed with grey or white
Liver – Red/brown
Points – Different coloured fur around the face, ears, feet and tail
Red Merle – Marbled red, white, and buff
Seal – Black with red cast in strong light
Wall eyes – One eye a different colour from the other
Wheaten – A pale yellow-beige colour